海伦·凯勒

Heroes and Role Models | Non-Fiction Series

Copyright © 2022 by Level Learning, INC. and Washington Yu Ying PCS™
Original and Edited Text Copyright © 2022 by Washington Yu Ying PCS™

All rights reserved. No part of this book in whole or part may be reproduced without written permission from the publisher.

Published by Level Learning, INC.

Content Contributors:
Washington Yu Ying PCS™
Level Learning - Ya-Ching Chang

Illustrations by: Josh Taira

Leveling classification based on Level Learning standard. For full description, visit www.levellearning.com

ISBN 978-1-64040-005-4
Simplified Chinese Edition

About Level Learning:
Level Learning provides a literacy focused curriculum specifically designed for K-12 Chinese as a Second Language classrooms. Our program offers 20 levels of specific and detailed objectives, leveled texts and passages, mastery-based online assessment, and analytics to enable data-driven instruction. Level Learning reading curriculum for both literature and informational text emphasize grammar and comprehension skills to help teachers develop confident and independent Chinese language readers. The non-fiction series of books are specifically designed to support our informational text course based on multiple national standards. To learn more about our entire offering, visit www.levellearning.com.

About Washington Yu Ying PCS™:
Washington Yu Ying PCS is a Mandarin English dual language immersion International Baccalaureate (IB) World school. Yu Ying's mission is to inspire and prepare young people to create a better world by challenging them to reach their full potential in a nurturing Chinese/English educational environment. Yu Ying's comprehensive IB, dual immersion curriculum equips students with global competencies for success in the real world. As a leader in immersion education, Yu Ying is determined to advance Chinese language programs and global citizenry education by helping other schools create and strengthen their Chinese programs. For more information, email: products@washingtonyuying.org

海伦·凯勒出生于1880年。她是一位著名的美国作家。

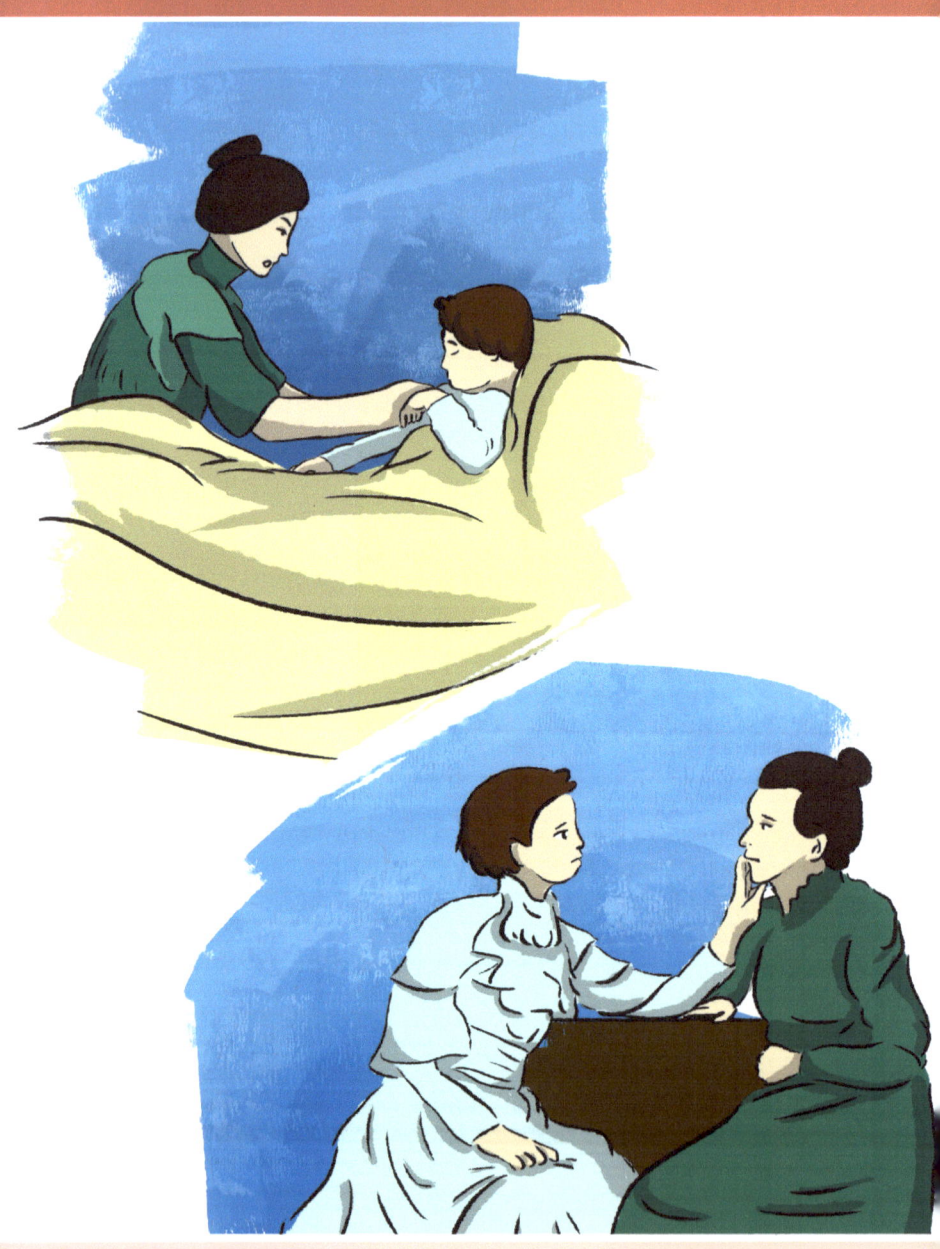

海伦·凯勒小时候生了一场病。这场病让她失去了听力和视力。因为听不见也看不到，所以她也不会说话。

长大以后,她知道自己和别人不一样,这让她常常感到生气和伤心。别人可以读书,但是她不能读书。别人可以说话,但是她不能说话。

别人的世界是彩色的，海伦·凯勒的世界却是一个黑色的、没有声音的地方。

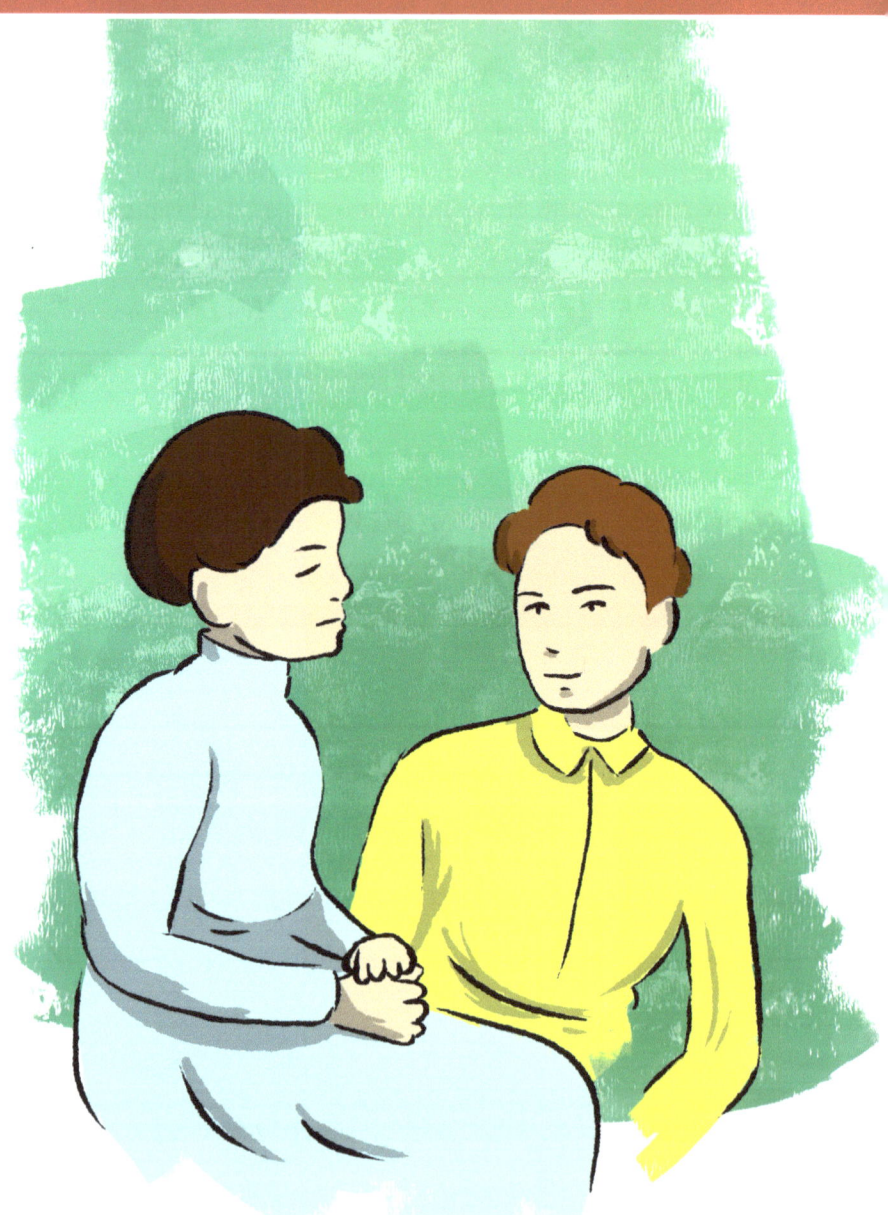

在海伦·凯勒七岁的时候,她的爸爸妈妈帮她找了一位老师。这位老师用了许多方法教她,可是海伦·凯勒都不明白。

有一天,这个老师带她出去玩水。老师把水洒到她的头上、脸上和手上,然后重复地把"水"这个字写在她的手上。这时候,海伦·凯勒知道了,原来老师写在她手上的字,就是"水"。

在老师的帮助下,海伦·凯勒学会了用盲人点字法来读书,也学会了说话。虽然她花了比别人更多的时间学习,但是她感到很开心。她觉得这个世界变成彩色的了!

长大以后,海伦·凯勒成为一位著名的作家。除了写书,她还到处演讲,因为她想要分享自己的故事来鼓励别人。

海伦·凯勒让大家知道，虽然盲人看不见，但是他们和正常人一样。盲人可以读书，盲人也可以做许多事情。

Glossary

	Pinyin	English Definition
著名	zhù míng	famous
作家	zuò jiā	writer
病	bìng	sickness
失去	shī qù	to lose
听力	tīng lì	hearing
视力	shì lì	vision, sight
世界	shì jiè	world
彩色	cǎi sè	color
声音	shēng yīn	sound
方法	fāng fǎ	method, way
明白	míng bai	to understand
洒	sǎ	to sprinkle, to spray
重复	chóng fù	to repeat
原来	yuán lái	turned out to be
盲人	máng rén	blind people

	Pinyin	English Definition
点字法	diǎn zì fǎ	Braille method
到处	dào chù	everywhere
演讲	yǎn jiǎng	to give speeches
分享	fēn xiǎng	to share
鼓励	gǔ lì	to encourage
正常	zhèng cháng	normal

www.ingramcontent.com/pod-product-compliance
Lightning Source LLC
Chambersburg PA
CBHW041223070526
44584CB00001B/65